My Dad, John McCain

MEGHAN McCAIN
ILLUSTRATED BY DAN ANDREASEN

ALADDIN

NEW YORK   LONDON   TORONTO   SYDNEY

ALADDIN

An imprint of Simon & Schuster Children's Publishing Division

1230 Avenue of the Americas, New York, NY 10020

Text copyright © 2008 by Meghan McCain

Illustrations copyright © 2008 by Dan Andreasen

Designed by Karin Paprocki

The text of this book is set in Adobe Garamond.

The illustrations are rendered in graphite on Bristol board and colored digitally.

Manufactured in the United States of America

First Aladdin Paperbacks edition September 2008

2 4 6 8 10 9 7 5 3 1

CIP data for this book is available from the Library of Congress.

ISBN-13: 978-1-4169-7528-1   ISBN-10: 1-4169-7528-4

INTREPID FALLEN HEROES FUND

The publisher shall donate one percent of its net proceeds from the sale of this book through regular U.S. trade channels to Intrepid Fallen Heroes Fund.

(Net proceeds are the gross amounts received by the publisher less shipping, mailing, and insurance costs or charges and taxes.)

Intrepid Fallen Heroes Fund is an organization that aids military personnel and veterans who have suffered severe traumatic brain injuries while serving our nation.

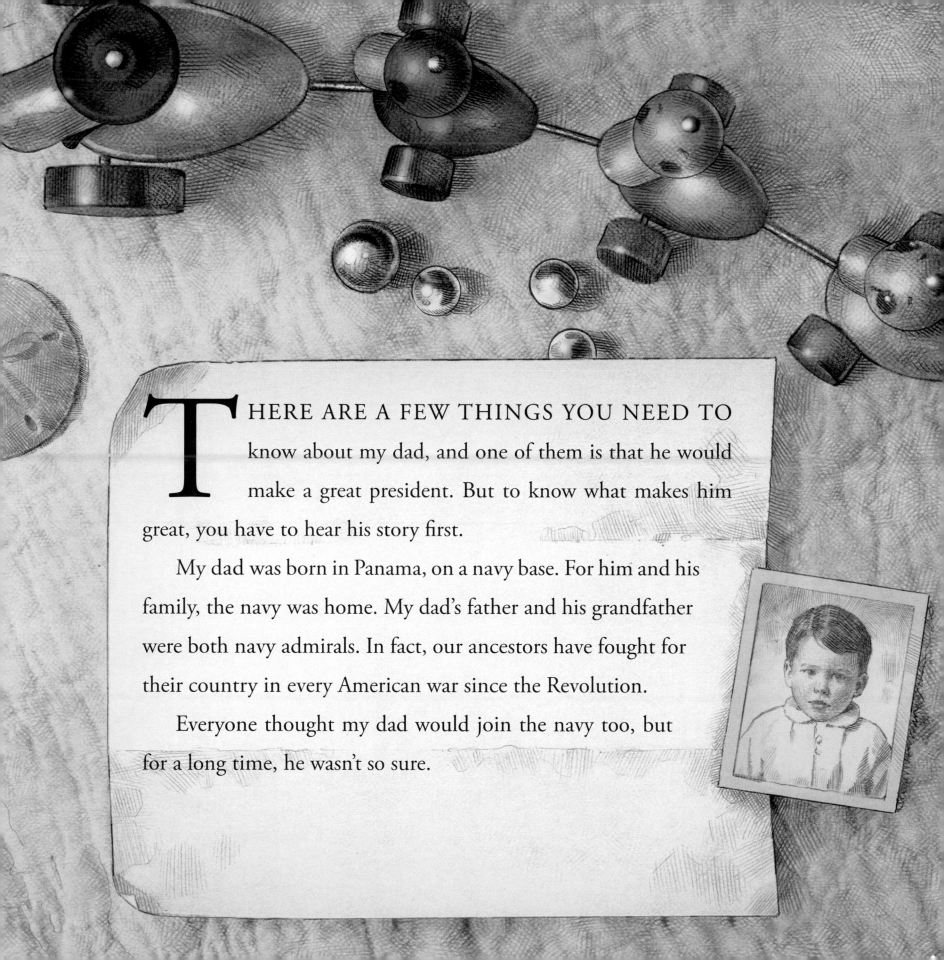

THERE ARE A FEW THINGS YOU NEED TO know about my dad, and one of them is that he would make a great president. But to know what makes him great, you have to hear his story first.

My dad was born in Panama, on a navy base. For him and his family, the navy was home. My dad's father and his grandfather were both navy admirals. In fact, our ancestors have fought for their country in every American war since the Revolution.

Everyone thought my dad would join the navy too, but for a long time, he wasn't so sure.

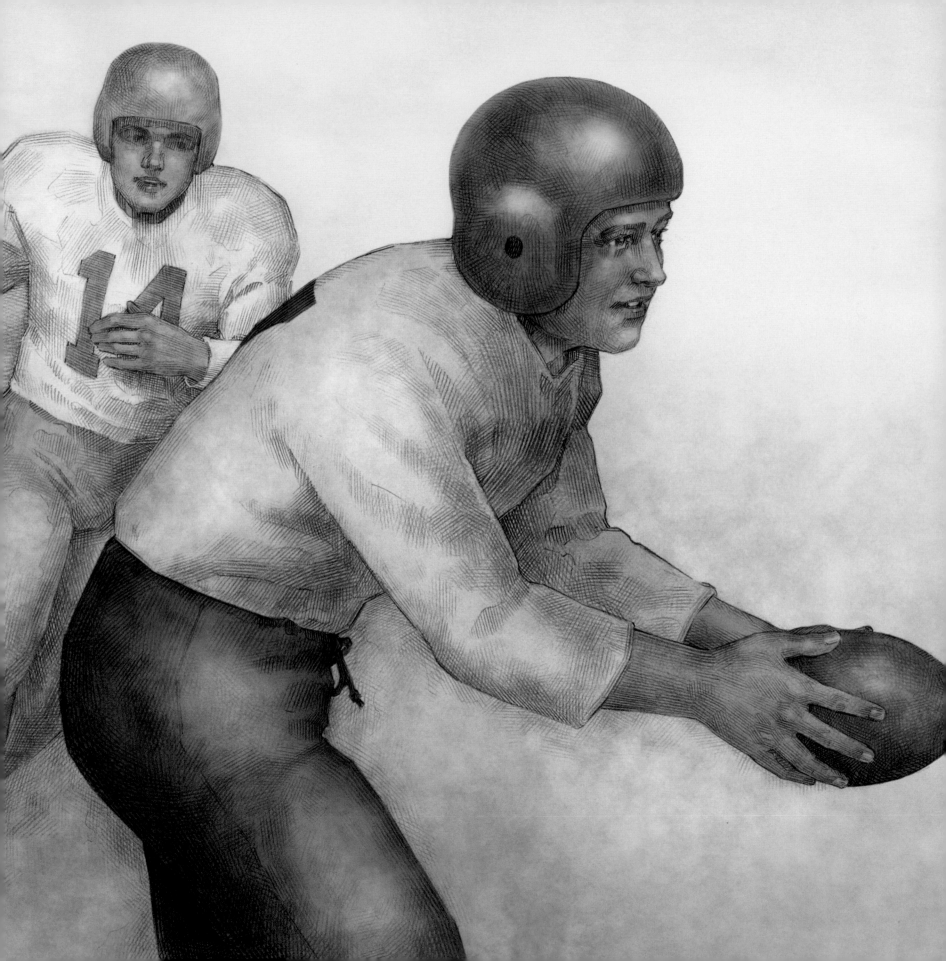

My father's family moved from naval base to naval base, which meant he switched schools all the time. Finally, when he was fifteen, he went to a boarding school in Virginia. He wasn't a very good student there. He broke a lot of rules, but he liked football and wrestling. He wasn't the biggest or the strongest guy on the football team—but he was one of the toughest. He just wouldn't give up.

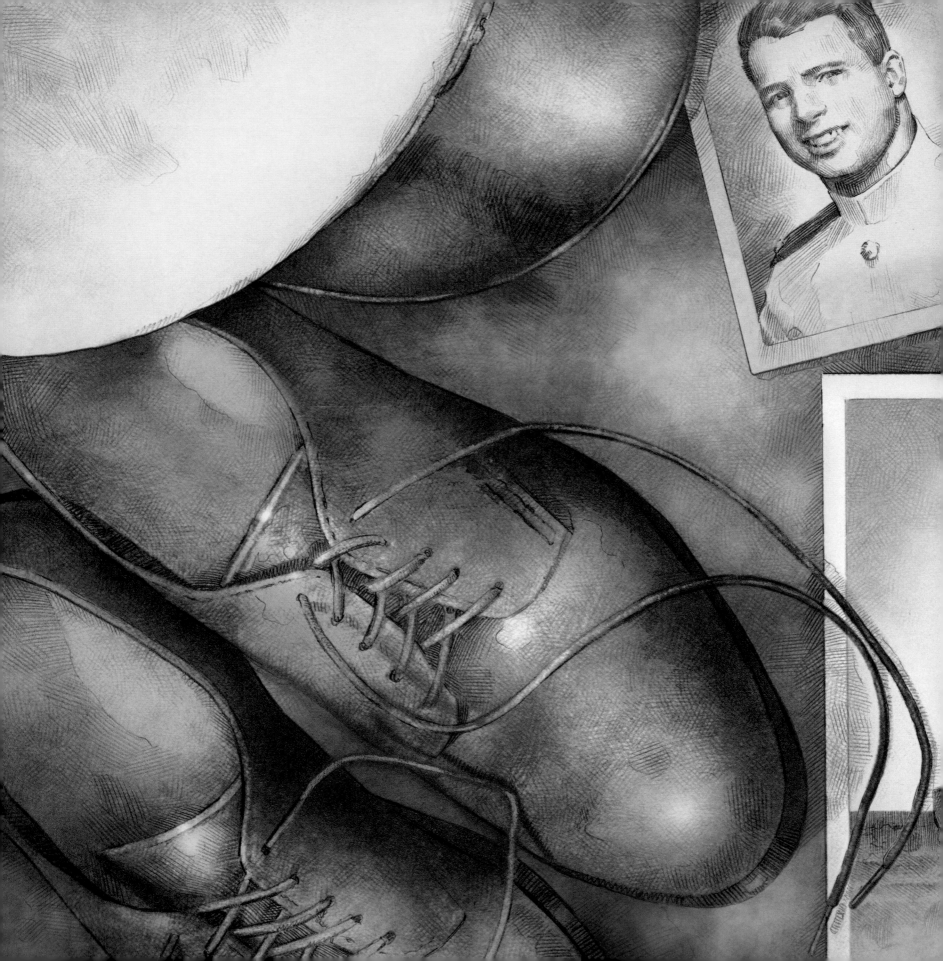

My grandparents knew my dad would go to the Naval Academy after high school. But at the Academy, you have to follow a lot of rules—and back then my dad wasn't so good at that! He didn't always keep his shoes shined or his room neat, and sometimes he even snuck out of school.

But when he went to sea on a practice training cruise, he liked it so much and did so well, his teachers were amazed. On a ship, following the rules kept things running smoothly—and he could see that was important for everyone.

The more my dad learned about life in the military, the more he knew he wanted to fly planes. After he graduated from the Academy, it was time for flight training. Learning to fly can be dangerous. Once, the engine of my dad's plane quit working and he crashed into a bay. He had to swim for his life.

But he still had his heart set on flying missions in the Vietnam War. He wanted to fight for his country, just like his father and grandfather. He wanted to do great things, just like them.

In Vietnam, my dad flew planes that took off from an aircraft carrier called the *Forrestal*. One day while he was waiting to take off, a bomb fell off another pilot's plane and smashed a fuel tank on my dad's plane. Fuel went everywhere, and pretty soon the whole ship was in flames.

My dad crawled out onto his plane's nose. He leaped through the flames and scrambled onto the deck. It's amazing he made it out alive. Bombs were exploding everywhere, and the fire burned all day and all night. It looked for sure like the *Forrestal* would sink, but the whole crew worked to save her—and they did.

Even after the *Forrestal* fire, my father kept flying. One October day he had to fly a very complicated mission. He had flown a lot of dangerous missions before, so he was sure he'd be okay on this one too.

But he wasn't.

He'd just dropped his bombs

on the target when a missile blew the right

wing off of his plane. The plane flew out of control,

and crashed. Luckily, my dad had parachuted out

and landed in a lake.

He was alive. But both his arms and one leg were broken, and

he'd been captured. He was now a prisoner of war.

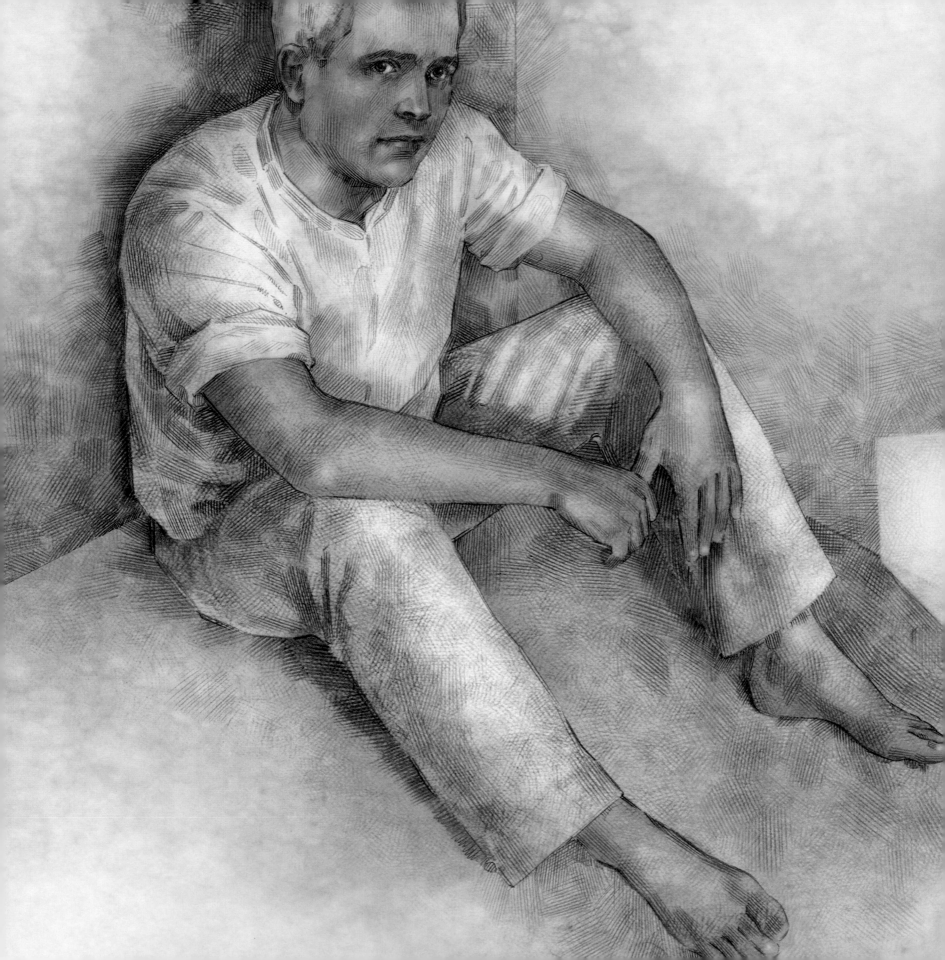

My dad and the other prisoners were treated badly. He didn't get the right kind of medical care for his broken bones, and the food was really bad—once he found a chicken foot in his lunch. But the prisoners did things to make themselves feel better. One guy sewed the American flag inside his pajamas. Every day they recited the Pledge of Allegiance.

But then my dad got a chance most prisoners didn't. Since he was an admiral's son, the Vietnamese who had captured him said they would let him go home. My dad was hurt, sick, and scared. But he knew there were some things more important than himself—like his faith in God, his country, and the men he served with. My dad wouldn't go home and leave his friends. I think only a great man would have made that choice.

So he said he'd only go home if everyone who'd been captured before him was set free too. And his captors said no. So my dad stayed in prison for five and a half years.

Finally, the war ended and my dad was set free.

He hardly knew anything about what had been happening in the world, although he did find out that while he was in Vietnam, astronauts had landed on the moon.

For everything he'd done in the navy, my dad earned the Silver Star, the Legion of Merit, the Distinguished Flying Cross, the Bronze Star, and the Purple Heart.

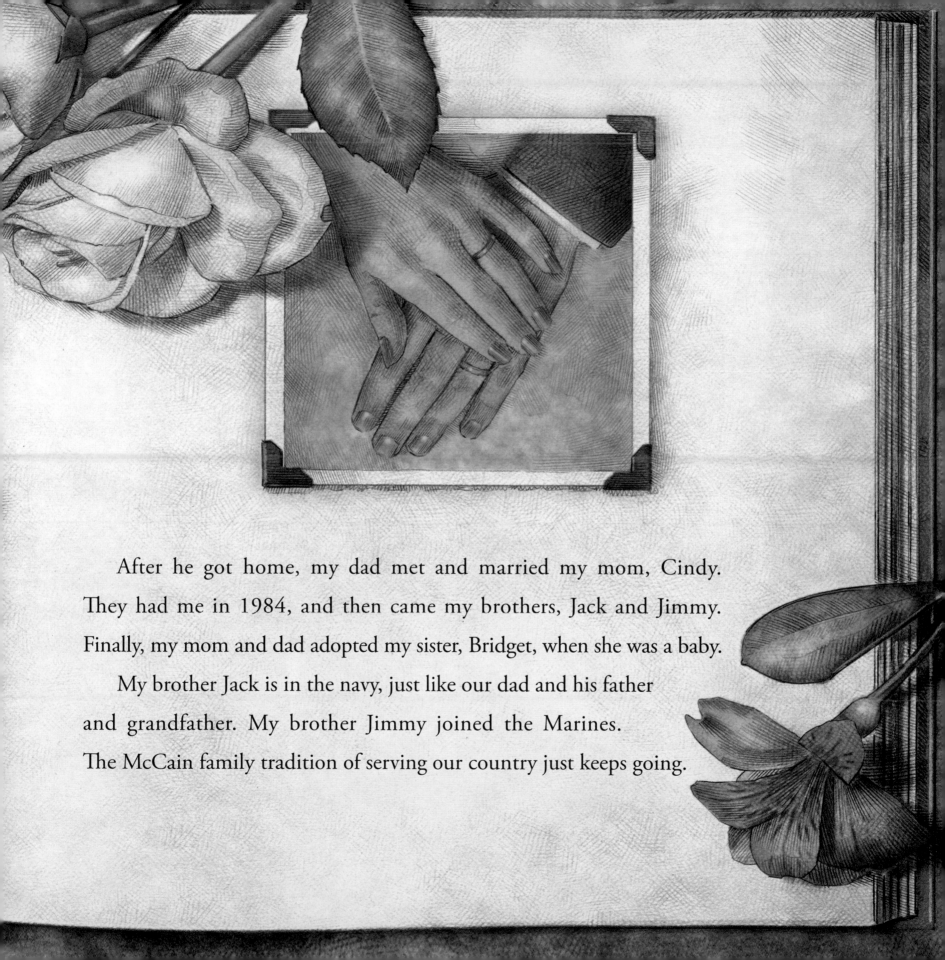

After he got home, my dad met and married my mom, Cindy. They had me in 1984, and then came my brothers, Jack and Jimmy. Finally, my mom and dad adopted my sister, Bridget, when she was a baby. My brother Jack is in the navy, just like our dad and his father and grandfather. My brother Jimmy joined the Marines. The McCain family tradition of serving our country just keeps going.

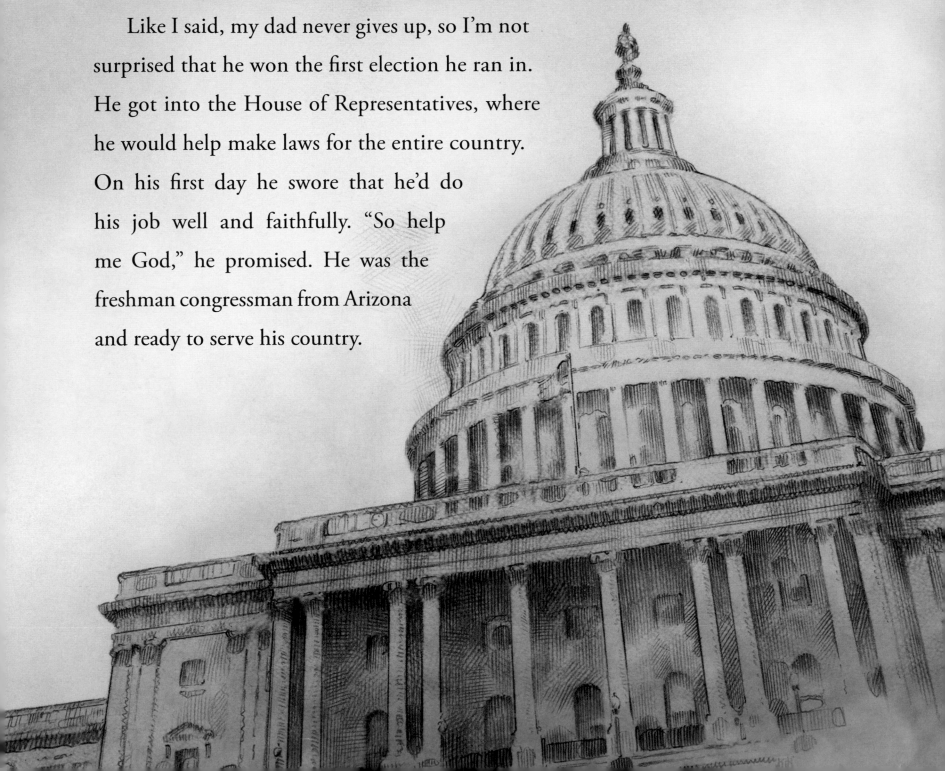

My dad stayed in the navy for a few more years, but he'd been so badly hurt, he wasn't able to fly a plane. So he began thinking about a new career—politics—and he moved to my mom's home state of Arizona.

Like I said, my dad never gives up, so I'm not surprised that he won the first election he ran in. He got into the House of Representatives, where he would help make laws for the entire country. On his first day he swore that he'd do his job well and faithfully. "So help me God," he promised. He was the freshman congressman from Arizona and ready to serve his country.

Dad's been in the U.S. Congress since I was a kid. But he wanted to do more.

He was always thinking about what he could do that would help his country.

I was a freshman in high school when my dad asked my brothers

and sister and me if we thought he should run for president in 2000.

After a family meeting, we all decided that it would be a good idea!

If you want to be president, first you have to be nominated by a political party. Then you run in the general election against the other candidates. My dad's a Republican, so he wanted the Republican Party to choose him.

He campaigned hard in 2000, and met a lot of people all over the country. But he didn't get enough votes to win the nomination. Still, he was proud of how hard he'd worked. And we were really proud of him too!

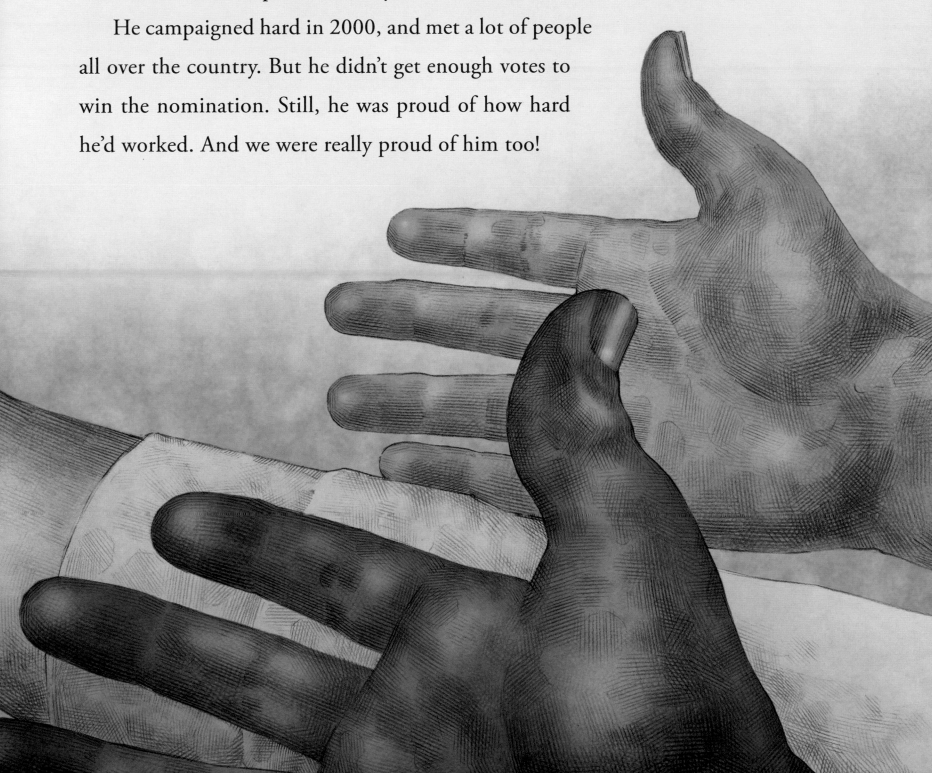

Some guys just don't quit. My dad is one of them.
Eight years later he decided to run for president again.
Things didn't look great at first. His campaign nearly ran
out of money. People were starting to say he didn't have
a chance.

But my dad never gives up. He kept talking to voters,
especially in the state of New Hampshire—meeting with
them, listening to them, joking with them, sometimes even
arguing with them. He wanted them to see what kind of
president he would make.

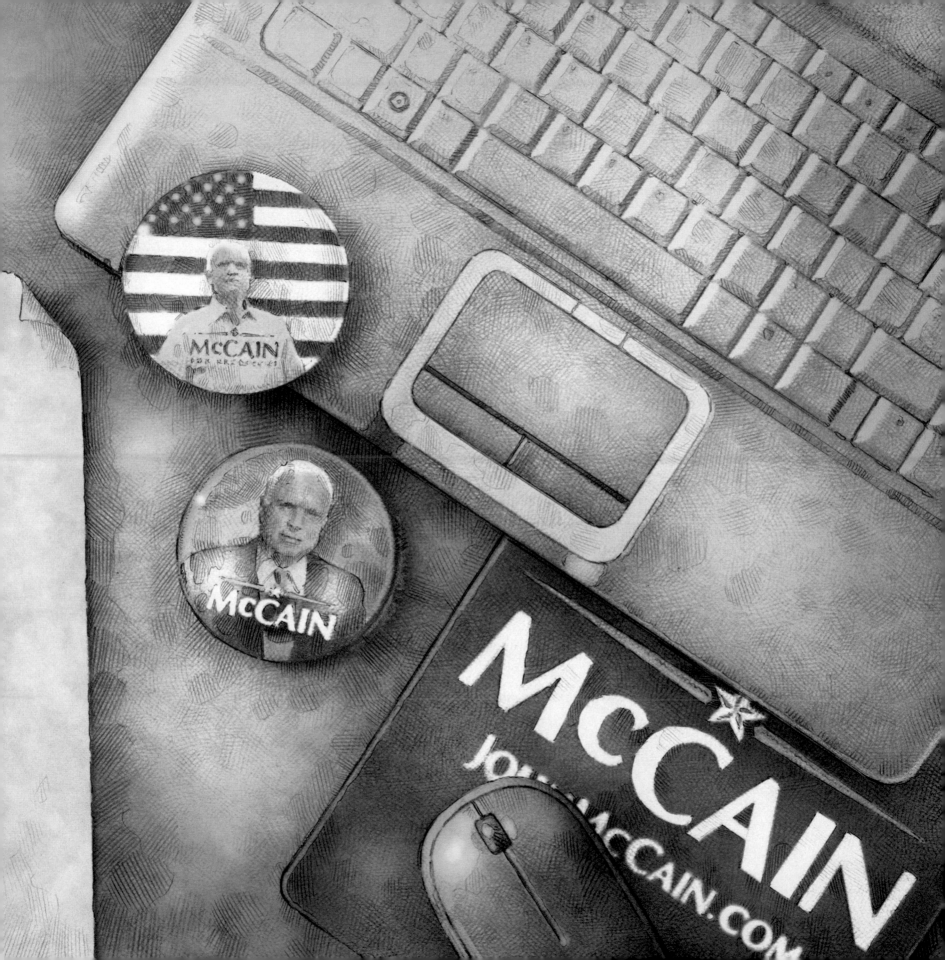

Voters in New Hampshire picked my dad as the Republican they wanted to run for president. Lots of other states picked him too. In September 2008, the Republican Party had a big meeting, the Republican National Convention. And on that day, my dad was officially chosen as the Republican candidate for president of the United States.

It takes a great man to be president of the United States, and I know that nobody will work harder than my dad to convince people that he's the right person for the job.

I also know he'll say what he really thinks. Maybe it won't always be what people want to hear. But it will be the truth.

And of course, my dad just doesn't give up. He never did when he was a prisoner of war, and I know that he never will give up fighting for what he believes in. And I'm sure of this—my father loves this country more than anyone I know. I love him for that.